Cover: Roger Liu

Second Edition, September 2015
Published in the United States by Enlight Press

Twitter.com/enlightpress
An imprint of *Enlight Foundation, Australia*

The First Paperback Edition of this Book was Published by
Ansarian Publications (Qom) in March 2015

MODARRESI, SAYED MAHDI
Twitter.com/SayedModarresi
Our Beliefs — Modarresi, Sayed Mahdi

BELIEFS; ISLAM; GOD; DOCTRINE; CREDENCE; CREED;
SHIA; RELIGION; FAITH; APOLOGETICS; POLEMICS; SCHO-
LASTIC THEOLOGY

D0817320

CONTENTS

WHY THIS BOOK?

This booklet is an edited, annotated, and abridged transcript of a series of lectures by the late Ayatollah Alamolhuda[1] The material contained herein is vital for today's youth; a generation thirsty for answers while facing an endless barrage of misconceptions and doubts. It is deliberately condensed to make it accessible to a wider audience; hence the synoptic form.

The discussions are designed to bolster our intellectual defenses and ensure the youth are protected against attacks to which they are constantly subjected.

It is also an introduction to the tenets of Islam and can help familiarize non-Muslims with the foundations of our faith.

It goes without saying that knowing the tenets of our religion is of critical importance. They form the bedrock of Islam, so much so that without a firm grounding in these beliefs none of our deeds have any value. Imam al-Baqer says:

---

1. See Appendix 1 for a brief look at the life of this great inspirational scholar

> *"No deed is of any benefit with rejection or doubt."*[2]

This is because our actions stem from our beliefs, hence the priority given to the establishment of an unshakable creed, to guard against confusion. This is also why the first question a person who leaves this world is asked is not about their acts of worship or their social standing, but *"Who is your Lord? Who is your apostle? Who is your leader? What do you believe in?"* This is why much of the Holy Quran and the words and sermons of Ahlulbayt are devoted to these pivotal matters of belief.

Consider this: In the heat of the battle of *Siffin*[3], while Imam Ali was faced with one of the most climacteric challenges against his authority, he stood to address his lieutenants when a Bedouin approached to ask a question. He said, *"O' Commander of the Faithful, do you claim that God is One?"*[4] Anyone else would have snubbed the stranger at once. At a time when the only pertinent topic was military strategy, tactical engagement with the enemy, and preventing its vicious onslaught, this man came asking a question entirely irrelevant. Against the backdrop of clamoring swords, terrifying cries of death, and limbs scattered across the sand dunes, this wandering villager wanted an answer to a seemingly inconsequential theological query!

Some companions raised their voices in protest, castigating the villager and demanding that the meeting stay focused on the crisis at hand. Upon seeing the commotion, Imam

---

2. Al-Kafi 2:400:7

«عن أَبِي جَعْفَرٍ عَلَيْهِ السَّلامُ قَالَ: لَا يَنْفَعُ مَعَ الشَّكِّ وَ الْجُحُودِ عَمَلٌ»

3. One of the first battles marking the Muslim 'civil wars' in which the authority of the Prophet's heir was challenged by the very same people who fought the Prophet himself.

4. قَالَ الأَعْرَابِي: يَا أَمِيرَ الْمُؤْمِنِينَ أَ تَقُولُ إِنَّ اللَّهَ وَاحِدٌ؟

Ali came to his defense, saying, "Leave him! What he seeks is precisely what we want from these people [our foes]."[5] Explaining that it is the rejection of God which has caused their enemy to behave the way it did, he proceeded to provide a detailed and nuanced response to the question[6]. It was a lesson for the troops to remember why they were at war, that their sacrifice meant something beyond patriotism or the euphoria of victory. It suggested the battles were not fought by Imam Ali in order to expand the empire or to seek conquest. It was a wake-up call that the defensive Jihad they were engaged in was to reclaim the freedom of those still shackled by ignorance; that matters of belief, especially those pertaining to God, are a step above even the most pressing crises; and there is no time or place where learning is in any way inapt. Imam Ali was trying to teach his men that the Bedouin's query had not just a peripheral correlation with the issue at hand – that of a battle between good and evil — but that it was directly connected to their just cause in its every detail.

The central role of our creed is demonstrated yet again in this prophetic narration:

> "*The example of this religion is like a firm tree; faith is its rootstock, prayer is its veins, almsgiving is its water, fasting is its fronds, morality is its leaves, and abstention from sins is its fruits. A tree is not complete without its fruit.*"[7]

The above narration demonstrates two key facts:

٥. قَالَ: دَعُوهُ فَإِنَّ الَّذِي يُرِيدُهُ الْأَعْرَابِيُّ هُوَ الَّذِي نُرِيدُهُ مِنَ الْقَوْمِ.

6. Al-Khisal 1:1, p.2 and Al-Tawheed 1:3, p.83

7. Bihar-ul-Anwar 79:213

First, the tenets of Islam are the foundation upon which all other acts are based. Much like a tree, they represent the roots, emphasizing their paramount position within the faith ecosystem.

Second, like branches, leaves, and fruits, acts of worship stem from this tree, and in turn, are based on established creed. In other words, while Islam's articles of faith are grounded in rationality (as shall be demonstrated in this book), the branches are rooted in pre-established beliefs and do not necessarily have a logical explanation other than their utility as a test of submission. Thus, basic beliefs such as the existence of God underpin others, building an elegant arborescent epistemic system, and constituting the touchstone for subsequent discussion.

Understanding this also sheds light on how the actions of some Muslims can be so divergent from the religion they profess. We can begin to answer such questions as, "How could a so-called 'Muslim' be so savage as to commit unspeakable acts of brutality?" or even "Why is it that an otherwise good Muslim is sinful?" A treelike approach means such inquiries correspond to the boughs, while the cause of the problem lies in the rhizome. In other words, something within the pages of the book you hold in your hand is amiss, leading to a malignant growth that disfigures a beautiful religion and turns it into an errant monstrosity.

I pray that God accepts this small deed from this destitute and reprehensible slave and redeems me on the Day of Judgment.

Mahdi al-Modarresi
Qom al-Muqaddasah
2015

PREAMBLE

It is a universally accepted fact that our fundamental beliefs must be founded *not* on treacly emotions or inherited dogma, but on the intellect[8]: that is to say, on intuitive, self-evident truths .[9]This is why Islam forbids believing in things not corroborated by or lacking in solid evidence .We also know that all people — from the most knowledgeable erudite down to the most illiterate savage — are equally obligated to seek the truth and recognize the purpose of their existence.

The evidence for God must, therefore, be both sound and uncomplicated in order to be within everyone's grasp and comprehension. It must not be contingent upon the

---

8. *Aql* (often translated as 'mind' or 'intellect') is the guiding light which illuminates our path and distinguishes right from wrong. It is the standard upon which humans test the truthfulness of any claim. It allows for substantiating the consistency, validity, soundness, and completeness of a premise. It encompasses the faculty of reasoning and understanding objectively, which fits squarely into our theology.

9. All wise people agree that the most reasonable approach to life's big questions is an evidential one. This requires that beliefs be based on sufficient evidence, leading up to self-evident, coherent truths.

acquisition of specialized knowledge, such as sophisticated philosophical arguments or mystical teachings. Everyone, from the learned to the unlettered, including all races, cultures, and creeds, must be able to understand and embrace the case for God once properly presented. This is based on the following three points:

1. Philosophy and mysticism are fields often inaccessible to those who lack the substantial intellectual capacity for these specialized fields, or those unwilling to dedicate the significant time and effort to become skilled in these disciplines.

2. Since everyone has a moral responsibility to know the truth,[10] they cannot afford to remain in the darkness of falsehood or doubt, even as they acquire the skills needed to understand philosophical or mystical arguments.

3. The methodologies employed by philosophers and mystics are erroneous, and they lead to a mythical 'god', one that falls within the grasp of human imagination and delusion. It is, after all, the product of imagination and delusion! On the other hand, prophets and their vicegerents seek to stimulate people's insights and awaken their innate experience of God. They attempt to rekindle the intellect through clear and unequivocal truths, leading them to acknowledge their Lord, who is beyond imagination, fantasy, or even the intellect's clench.

The Commander of the Faithful, Imam Ali, speaks of the role of prophets in this regard:

---

10. The obligation to seek the truth stems from epistemic justification. The only other alternatives are ignorance and belief in falsehood, none of which is rationally valid.

> *"Then Allah sent His Messengers and series of His prophets towards them to get them to fulfill the pledges of His creation, to recall to them His bounties, to exhort them by preaching, to unearth before them the hidden virtues of their intellects and show them the signs of His Omnipotence"*[11]

Thus, this is the approach that we will take in establishing our beliefs.

---

11. Nahjul Balagha, Sermon One, 'Allah chooses His Prophets'

Part One

THE CREATOR

The bedrock of Islam and the purpose of all creation — knowing the Creator — is the singular foundation of all divine faiths. This subject, while much debated, is simple at its core and is presented in this book in a way that everyone can comprehend and begin to appreciate the splendor of connecting with the very source of our existence.

There are two ways by which we can prove the Creator:

1. REASON

Everything has an origin and a point at which it did not exist. And since things have a beginning, it is logically unsound and simply irrational for them to exist without an external agent which brings it about. Anyone endowed with the faculty of reason or even a modicum of intelligence, upon seeing something that was not and then was, would seek its creator. If you see a small computer that has power-

ful new features never before seen, the first question you will
ask is, *who invented this?* When a new scientific discovery is
announced, the discoverers are concurrently acknowledged
and their achievements honored. When you see a work of
art that takes your breath away, you automatically search for
the artist behind the art.

Common sense tells us that everything was preceded
with a state of nonexistence. Then, one after another, they
came into being, with impeccable order, design, and symmetry clearly visible and dominant in all things. It is our
faculty of reason which guides us towards a wise and powerful creator who designed and created them. The Quran
reminds us of this fact by asking rhetorically, "*Or were they
created out of naught? Or are they the creators?*"[12]

The fact that humans did not exist at some point, then
came into being, is an obvious and established fact. Therefore, how can we say that this awe-inspiring, sensational
creature either came into being without a creator — a prop-
osition rejected by reason — or that we created ourselves
— yet another absurd assumption, for how could we create
ourselves or cause anything to be before we even existed?
It also makes no sense to say man created himself after he
came into existence, because that which exists does not need
to be brought into existence.[13]

Therefore, all that exists in the universe has been brought
into being by an omniscient, omnipotent creator, whom we

12. Quran 52:35

﴿أَمْ خُلِقُوا مِنْ غَيْرِ شَيْءٍ أَمْ هُمُ الْخَالِقُونَ﴾

13. Appealing to the theory of evolution is also not a valid logical position because in addition to the structural deficiencies it has in explaining the complexity
of life, none of the assumptions it makes account for existence itself. In other
words, it fails to answer the basic question, 'why there is something rather than
nothing?'.

must seek with utmost devotion and sincerity so we can achievesuccess.[14]

2. BY NATURAL DISPOSITION

Humans are created in such a way that, under certain conditions, they fully acknowledge a wise and powerful Creator who is in control of their affairs. In other words, mankind is cognizant of the power and authority of God within himself. He does this by contemplating the fact that he was not and now he is, that he was young and is now grown up, that he was a vulnerable child and is now a strong youth. The transition then continues back into weakness and fragility as he ages. He might also contemplate that he was well then became sick, or was sick and became well, or he was angry and became satisfied, or was satisfied then became angry, or that he was sad then happy, or happy then

---

14. Logically speaking, there are only three possible scenarios as to the origin of the universe: A) The natural universe has existed forever exerting work and burning as a perpetual motion machine; or, B) The universe created itself, so to speak, i.e., come into existence apart from an external source; or, C) The universe was created by an external source outside of the natural universe, i.e., a supernatural Creator; There is no logical fourth alternative. Either the natural universe was always here, or it popped into existence by itself from nothing, or a supernatural creator made it.

sad.[15] The very fact that we find much to be beyond our control reminds us of the existence of a deity who exercises full authority over our lives as well as the world at large.

Likewise, when man falls into a predicament so difficult that to reach deliverance he severs hope from all conventional means, at that precise moment when he recognizes his arrant deficiency and feels his inherent destitution and complete helplessness, he also discovers the limitless power of God, to whom he extends his hand, beseeching Him for help and salvation.

A man said to Imam al-Sadeq: "Guide me to God and [show me] who He is, for I am confused by those who argue."

Imam al-Sadeq said, "Have you ever boarded a ship?"

"Yes," said the man.

"Have you found yourself shipwrecked and in a state [of despair] where no boat can salvage you and no swimming can avail you?" continued the Imam.

"Yes," said the man.

---

15. Imam al-Sadeq said to Ibn Abil Awjaa: Woe unto you! How could the one who has demonstrated his power within you, be veiled from you? [He does so in] your non-existence before you were, your growth following your youth, your strength after your frailty, your frailty after your strength, your sickness after your health, your health after your sickness.. Your love after your hatred, your hatred after your love, your acceptance after your refusal, your refusal after your acceptance, your desire after your contempt, your contempt after your desire, your fear after trust, your trust after your fear, your hope after your despair, your despair after your hope, the spark of what you did not even imagine, and forgetting what was stored in your memory... Ibn Abil Awjaa said "he went on stating the things which point to His power right within me, things that I cannot drive away from myself, that I thought God was about to appear between him and I".Al- Tawheed, al-Sadouq p.127

"Did your heart then recognize that there must be something that can save you from your plight?" the Imam asked.

The man replied in the affirmative yet again.

Imam al-Sadeq then said, "That 'thing' is God, who is able to save where there is none which can save, and can rescue where there is no one who can rescue."[16]

Of course, it is possible that innate desires such as lust, anger, love of power, will overrun man's natural inclination, and obscure the presence of God. However, at times of utter despair, when calamity strikes and difficulty erupts such that all hope is lost, this natural intuition reveals itself once again and guides us towards our powerful, self-sufficient Lord. At that moment, desires and animalistic inclinations cease to function, restoring our 'self' to its original purity whereby we can see the truth. We thus have a chance to succumb to God and repent to him by seeking refuge in Him, seeking Him alone for salvation and help.

It is during these moments of distress in one's life that we awaken from distraction and negligence. At times of trial and tribulation, humans discover God, fully acknowledge His existence, and bow down before His majesty.[17] This

---

16. al-Sadouq Al-Tawheed, 231

17. Fitrah (فطرة), is an Arabic word meaning '*disposition*', '*constitution*', and is loosely related to '*instinct*'. It refers to innate beliefs, intuitions, or insights. Other religions also believe in an innate knowledge which acts as a moral compass. The Calvinist term *Sensus divinitatis* or the Buddhist *Dzogchen*, meaning the natural, primordial state, all refer to a similar concept. Islam suggests human beings are born with an innate familiarity with God, encapsulated in *fitrah*. Along with compassion, intelligence, kindness and other attributes, it epitomizes what it is to be human. It is for this reason that some Muslims refer to those who embrace Islam as *reverts* rather than *converts*, as it is believed they are returning to this pure, natural state of submission to the Creator. It is precisely this *fitra* which is awakened by circumstances of immense fear or distress.

experience of the Divine is not mediated by intellectual and cognitive activity. Irrespective of the specific teachings and practices of a specific tradition, those who undergo this experience acquiesce to the sublime grandeur of the Creator.

Part Two

MONOTHEISM

After looking carefully at the previous two arguments, which dealt with the existence of the omnipotent, omniscient, sagacious, and sublime Creator, it becomes clear that there is no real need to prove His 'oneness'. Any sensible and intelligent person, who becomes aware of the absolute wisdom and power of the Creator, also recognizes His oneness and absolute uniqueness. When trials and tribulations strike like a hurricane, shaking the proverbial ship and those in it, thus severing their hope from everything and everyone, they all turn to Him and invoke Him. They will plead for His help and pray with utmost sincerity. When they cry and sob, beseeching Him for intervention, they will know in their hearts and minds that it is He and He alone who can save them from that which afflicts them. In such grueling circumstances, where God's existence becomes a certainty, His oneness is also established connotatively and without a shadow of doubt, rendering any proof redundant.

Conversely, mystics and philosophers often try to prove

God's existence, and then attempt to prove his oneness. In other words, they tackle the matter in two stages: first they argue (through causality, etc.) that a 'god' exists. They then endeavor to establish Oneness and lay the arguments for it. The Holy Quran, however, presents monotheism as a holistic and an undeniable fact: "Can there be doubt concerning Allah, the Creator of the heavens and the earth?"[18] Upon close inspection, it becomes clear that the verse establishes both the Creator as well as His oneness, all with one simple rhetorical question.

Therefore, the evidence for the oneness of the Lord encompasses the evidence for the wise and powerful Creator. This means that the intellect and our natural disposition (discussed in the previous section) are proofs for the oneness of the Creator as well as His existence.

To clarify this further we can address this issue from different perspectives, but for the interest of being brief, we will refer to three points:

1. A partner, in the sense of one who provides help and assistance, is obviously rejected in the Divine. Partnerships, by definition, connote a mutual deficiency. They apply where one wants to carry out a task but cannot do so alone, and so seeks assistance, the help, knowledge, power, or influence of another. Therefore, a partnership in any task is a sign of weakness and lack, in either skill, funds, or ability.

By carefully observing the multitudes of creatures and the sheer size and complexity of the universe, we find unmistakable proof that the Creator is knowledgeable, and that His power and meticulous skill is limitless. This im-

---

18. Quran 14:10

﴿قَالَتْ رُسُلُهُمْ أَ فِي اللهِ شَكٌّ فَاطِرِ السَّمَاوَاتِ وَ الْأَرْضِ يَدْعُوكُمْ لِيَغْفِرَ لَكُمْ مِنْ ذُنُوبِكُمْ وَ يُؤَخِّرَكُمْ إِلَى أَجَلٍ مُسَمًّى قَالُوا إِنْ أَنْتُمْ إِلاَّ بَشَرٌ مِثْلُنا تُرِيدُونَ أَنْ تَصُدُّونا عَمَّا كانَ يَعْبُدُ آباؤُنا فَأْتُونا بِسُلْطانٍ مُبِينٍ﴾

measurably wise and powerful God needs no partners, for that would mean He is weak and deficient, be it in His knowledge (thus, requiring Him to seek the advice of a more knowledgeable partner), or in His power (thus, forcing Him to procure the help of a more powerful being). He who needs the help of another — however small that need — cannot possibly be the Creator of this vast, intricate, and spectacular creation.

2. Evidence from order and design. Upon interacting with variegated creatures, we become fully cognizant that each of them is supported by a purposive order, from the motion of celestial bodies to the rotation of the earth, producing the succession of day and night and the transition of the four seasons, as well as the impeccable order and efficiency of bodily organs. These are but some of the things which highlight the systematic and structured nature of the world. Even where there is apparent chaos, there still remains temporal order and design. This order in all things and the beauty of the world, whether mathematically elegant or ineffably complex, is pronounced evidence of the knowledgeable, powerful, and wise Creator.

Upon closer examination, we discover something even more profound: that as far as science has been able to progress, there appears to be a link presiding over all things, creating a flawless harmony, a common thread, and a purposive system that underpins all natural functions. For instance, rain and snow falls from the sky, nourishing the earth with water, which enables vegetation to grow, which in turn purifies the air, allowing people and animals to breathe, saturating their blood with oxygen, making body functions healthy, and life continues with the consumption of plants and animals, as well as the production of drugs and medications to heal ailments. Food is consumed through the mouth, which has four types of teeth: incisors at the front, which cut the food; the canine, in the corners of the mouth, designed for grasping and tearing the food; premolars, located behind the canine and are meant for crushing food; and molars, the last teeth, whose job is to chew and grind the food into smaller pieces. The mouth releases a special enzyme from the salivary glands which helps prepare the food for digestion. A dedicated passageway directs the food into the stomach, which breaks down and processes it before releasing its nutrients into the bloodstream. The pristine cohesion, harmony, and organization to which we have alluded to is yet another sign of its maker, much like an orderly school with its organized classes and methodical syllabus points to a wise and orderly governor/principal.

The harmonious nature of the universe, the universal nature of the laws of physics, the regularity and consistency of the state of affairs points to one undeniable, indisputable, unquestionable, self-evident fact: that the world we observe around us is the product of a wise, and omnipotent creator. [19]

3. Evidence from natural disposition. Just as human disposition serves to prove the Creator, it also serves to prove His oneness. When mankind realizes his inherent poverty, and severs hope from all natural means and material agencies, he turns to the One who knows his need and is capable

---

19. Skeptics and atheists often posit that science explains the order in the world, but that would be to miss the point of the argument. Science tells us just how orderly the universe is (thus confirming the teleological argument for the existence of God) and attempts to express the symmetry in terms of scientific laws, but what needs explaining is the scientific laws themselves. In other words, what requires an explanation is why the world is like that in the first place, why it is such that it can be described by scientific laws, why there are laws instead of utter chaos? There are not scientific question as they are grand questions which fall outside the scope of modern experimental or even theoretical science.

of satisfying it: the Lord who saves the destitute from affliction, and our souls from extinction. Man turns to one singular point, and his heart clings to a sole entity; the object of devotion to whom all others turn at times of tribulation.

Part Three

DIVINE JUSTICE

One of the tenets of our creed is the principle of God's justice and that He does not oppress. To better understand this concept it is crucial to correctly define the term 'justice' and its antonym.

The noun 'justice' is often defined as the quality of being fair and reasonable. But from an Islamic perspective, it is simply 'to do the right thing'. Thus, to act justly is *to do that which must be [or is better] done*. Conversely, 'injustice' is *to do the wrong thing* or 'that which must not be done'. This illustrates how vastly inclusive these terms are. While in the English language, the word 'injustice' typically means to infringe on other people's rights, in Arabic, the term refers to every deviant thought, false belief, odious act, as well as behavior which violates the rights of others. And while the word 'justice' may denote a sense of equality, a more thorough inspection reveals that equal treatment among everyone is not always 'right' or 'fair'. For example, if a teacher gave equal grades to all his students, this equity among hard working and lazy pupils will be seen as wrong and, therefore, it is unjust. Everyone would agree that this is a gross miscarriage of justice and in contravention of fairness (which is to act appropriately in the circumstances). Therefore, justice and equality are not necessarily synonymous.

With that established, the principle of justice attributed to God refers to Him not doing 'that which must not be done' or 'that which is inappropriate'. It means that everything originates from God — from creation, to the legal framework for life, as well as the punitive measures designed to enforce the law — is appropriate and praiseworthy.

JUSTICE IN CREATION

Divine justice is also visible within matters of creation. While the detailed discussions fall beyond this work, it is worth mentioning the following points:

Firstly, insofar as humankind has been able to understand the wonders of creation, it is abundantly clear that everything is where it is supposed to be. Much like the position of the eyes, mouth, nose, and eyebrows, the entire universe seems to be exactly where it is intended to be. Everything from the cosmological constant (which suggests fine-tuning in the most staggering sense) to the infinitesimal details of nature is absolutely perfect. Everything is governed by an intricate and marvelous system. While the universe is sure to have many more deep secrets yet to be discovered, science has not been able to show a single creature or object which demonstrates a lack good judgment or one that is completely aimless and futile.

Secondly, to oppress and commit injustice is to exhibit a sign of either ignorance or impotence (or both). One who knows both the hideous nature of evil and has the power to achieve his objectives, has no reason to be unjust. In addition, by merely observing matter in this universe we reach this irrefutable conclusion: the Creator is both potent and all-knowing, meaning He has no deficiency of any kind that would compel Him into treating his creation with even the slightest hint of inequity.

Furthermore, God has endowed mankind with free will and the ability to make our decisions without coercion. Through prophets and messengers, He has shown us the path to righteousness and how we can descend into evil. To steer us in the right direction, he promised reward for doing good and warned of punishment for committing evil. "*Then anyone who has done an atom's weight of good, shall see it! And anyone who has done an atom's weight of evil, shall see it*"[20]

Moreover, God commands us to be just, saying "Lo! Allah enjoins justice and kindness,"[21] and "Verily Allah will not deal unjustly with man in aught; it is man that wrongs his own soul."[22] How could Allah, who himself commands us to be just and avoid wronging others, commit even the faintest act of injustice?

Let us briefly respond to the so-called 'Problem of Evil'. Imagine a three-year old child being given a bitter medi-

---

20. Quran 99:6-7

﴿فَمَنْ يَعْمَلْ مِثْقَالَ ذَرَّةٍ خَيْراً يَرَهُ * وَ مَنْ يَعْمَلْ مِثْقَالَ ذَرَّةٍ شَرًّا يَرَهُ﴾

21. Quran 16:90

﴿إِنَّ اللهَ يَأْمُرُ بِالْعَدْلِ وَ الْإِحْسَانِ وَ إِيتَاءِ ذِي الْقُرْبَى وَ يَنْهَى عَنِ الْفَحْشَاءِ وَ الْمُنْكَرِ وَ الْبَغْيِ يَعِظُكُمْ لَعَلَّكُمْ تَذَكَّرُونَ﴾

22. Quran 10:44

﴿إِنَّ اللهَ لَا يَظْلِمُ النَّاسَ شَيْئاً وَلَكِنَّ النَّاسَ أَنْفُسَهُمْ يَظْلِمُونَ﴾

cine. The child will naturally resist taking the drug as she sees no conceivable purpose for taking something which is unpleasant. Given that recovery does not usually occur instantaneously, a doctor struggles in making the case that the medicine is intended to relieve a pain or help the child recuperate. From the child's perspective, taking the drug is wrong and forcing her to take it is unjust. But if the ill child had the mental capacity to see the bigger picture, and more information about the drug's quality, things would be different. In fact, from her parent's perspective, the pain of the injection or the bitterness of the drug is a necessary evil. Not giving their daughter that antibiotic — however painful it is for her to endure and for the parents to watch — is the real evil. In much the same way, pain and misery in this world, especially those caused by natural phenomenon, while painful, and which must be averted if possible, is negligible, given that this life is a transient and minuscule part of the afterlife.

Part Four

COERCION & DELEGATION

Following the discussion of divine justice, it is pertinent to address the topic of free will.[23] After some contemplation on the matter, a number of issues become evident:

1. We find that the knowledge and power that we possess are not self-acquired, but attained from another. That is because every knowledgeable and able person is, at the time of his or her birth, both impotent and ignorant. With the passage of time, s/he acquires knowledge and increases in strength, and then enters a phase of old age characterized by frailty and feeble-mindedness. S/he even forgets information that s/he had attained in his/her youth and would otherwise be obvious to him/her. This is proof that the fac-

---

23. Although this subject is not typically discussed within the sphere of fundamental matters of belief, the teacher saw it fitting, albeit briefly, given that doubts may arise upon discussing divine justice. He is not attempting to cite every theory and engage in a polemic debate. Rather, he makes logical assertions consistent with Islamic Twelver creed in a way that makes the otherwise complex subject accessible to all.

ulties of reason and physical strength are acquired traits, bestowed upon us by the glorious Creator through various means, not ourselves.

2. The ability to make choices – that is, having the intellectual freedom to make decisions, and then proceed with executing those decisions – is something we can all sense.[24] Whether good or bad, it is 'I' who makes choices, and human beings have recognized this reality since time immemorial. This is why in every society there are laws that govern human affairs and anyone violating those laws is penalized for their actions. These very laws are proof that we exercise free will, for if we did not have the ability to choose for ourselves, being bound by the law would be absurd. Punishment for violating the law means man has the ability to make decisions freely. Otherwise, it is preposterous to punish someone for having done things involuntarily or out of coercion.

If a student has no choice in fulfilling his duties and learning, it would be wrong for the teacher to impose those duties. Likewise, if a hard-working student and a lazy one were both forced, and neither had the freedom to choose to study, it would be a mistake to distinguish between the two. Similarly, if a patient could not take his medicine and follow the prescription (due to a mental disability, for instance), the doctor would be misguided in giving a prescription in the first place, because he who has no choice, cannot be obligated to make that choice.

Thus, we are fully cognizant of the fact that we have both

---

24. Despite a plethora of influences, our choices are self-determined, that is to say, we determine what decisions we make. This does not deny that outside forces can influence or even severely limit the choices we make, but in the end, we still make a choice.

the power and the freedom to make decisions, and are not subject to coercion in our actions. We also realize that this power and freedom is bestowed upon us by our Creator and is not of our own making. Imam al-Redha said, "He is the owner of what He has let them own, and He is enabler of what He has enabled them to do."[25]

In other words, He, the exalted, has made us in possession of power and freedom, so He is more in possession of these faculties than we are. Moreover, because He is the giver of all faculties, He may strip us of them whenever He wishes to do so.

Therefore, because the full power to choose what we do has been endowed to us, allowing us to choose good deeds or bad deeds, we are under '*No Coercion*'. Because it is God who gives His slaves the faculties of power and freedom to choose and can take them at His discretion, we possess '*No Delegation*', hence the narration which states: '*No coercion, and no delegation, but a state between the two*'.

We are all fully aware of the fact that we are not coerced in the decisions that we make or the actions that we perform. While we may feel compelled do certain things (we go to work because we have to make a living, or go to school to graduate, etc.), in the end, we make a conscious, free decision to move forward or refrain. No amount of outside influence can coerce us into anything. At the same time, we are also intrinsically aware that we have no delegation in our decisions either. We are cognizant of our dependence upon the Creator who gives us all the faculties needed to carry out tasks, including willpower. That sense of awareness

---

25. al-Sadouq, al-Tawheed, 361

عن الرضا عليه السلام: إِنَّ اللَّهَ عَزَّ وَ جَلَّ لَمْ يُطَعْ بِإِكْرَاهٍ وَ لَمْ يُعْصَ بِغَلَبَةٍ وَ لَمْ يُهْمِلِ الْعِبَادَ فِي مُلْكِهِ هُوَ الْمَالِكُ لِمَا مَلَّكَهُمْ وَ الْقَادِرُ عَلَى مَا أَقْدَرَهُمْ عَلَيْهِ

is further heightened when we lose those faculties, such as when we fall asleep or when we die. This means what I possess, I possess only because someone gave me those abilities, hence the fact that they come and go.

Part Five

PROPHETHOOD

In order for mankind to prosper and for the purpose of creation to be fulfilled, there is a critical, inalienable need for a divine legal structure to be revealed to us.[26] However, to complement the theoretical aspect, God sends prophets as guides and mentors.

We can deduce the necessity for this from a multitude of avenues, especially in light of the following considerations:

1. Evidently, man is a social creature and solitary life without any human interaction is simply impossible. In order to satisfy our basic needs, be it for food, clothing, housing, or health, we need to live within a communal framework.

2. Obviously, for society to survive and function in an orderly fashion, it needs to be governed by a sound set of

26. This part is not interested in the political structure of society, nor the role of religion in government, or the extent to which state affairs can intersect with faith. Rather, we are dealing with moral theory and the position of religion in individual and social life. Those highly technical topics should be addressed in more in-depth, specialized settings.

laws and regulations. This is why every society, regardless of race or creed — even a strictly secular system — is bound by law. This is applicable in all social structures, including such fields as management and manufacturing where individual units operating within these fields must abide by regulations to ensure efficiency and compliance. Even the smallest social units cannot escape the need for laws that govern its activities.

3. A sound and valid law is one that conforms to the purpose and function of its host, and is compatible with the nature of man. Just like a washing machine, for which there is a method suitable to assemble and use, the design specifications by which the device was manufactured dictate how it must be operated.

4. No one is more capable of producing a law that suits our nature than our Creator. He knows our needs and is fully aware of what harms and what benefits us. The incontrovertible truth is that the creator of any given thing knows its secrets, needs, features, and vulnerabilities better than anybody else. Using the previous example, the team of designers, engineers, and manufacturers who collectively create the washing machine produce a set of instructions in the form of a manual to illustrate the best practices of handling the device. Like the machine's designer, the Creator of humanity alone is capable of setting the program for their social and individual lives.

5. So long as nature remains consistent and the human condition stays unchanged (our basic instincts, desires, and needs are essentially the same throughout the ages), the law that governs humankind also stays unchanged. Just as in the previous example, so long as the manufacturer introduces no major changes to the device, so too remain the laws that

govern it. "There is no alteration to God's creation."[27] Thus, the law of the Messenger of God remains intact, for it is the final law.

Those who argue that times — and therefore living conditions — have changed, and that lifestyles today are starkly different from what they were in bygone times, suggesting that laws must be amended, fail to take into account a very important fact. Indeed, man's lifestyle in terms of the means and accessories we use to make a living have changed. This includes such things as food, clothing, accommodation, transportation, communication, medicine, and technology, many of which could — and certainly will —continue to evolve in the future. However, the man of today and the man of yesterday and tomorrow are essentially the same as far as their basic needs are concerned. We have already established that the law has to match the needs of humanity, not their means and accessories with which those needs are met.

It is worth noting that our divinely-appointed leaders have stipulated a degree of elasticity in some aspects of religion. They have done so by making references to certain matters in a partial and specific manner, while at other times, they have elaborated on them in a general sense. An expert in the field of religion — i.e. a qualified jurist — can extrapolate rules that suit each given time from those broad principles.

So to sum up, humans need to maintain order in their lives, and to do that they require a constitution devised by the Creator, and for that constitution to be delivered to

---

27. Quran 30:30

﴿فَأَقِمْ وَجْهَكَ لِلدِّينِ حَنِيفاً فِطْرَتَ اللهِ الَّتِي فَطَرَ النَّاسَ عَلَيْهَا لا تَبْدِيلَ لِخَلْقِ اللهِ ذلِكَ الدِّينُ الْقَيِّمُ وَ لكِنَّ أَكْثَرَ النَّاسِ لا يَعْلَمُونَ﴾

them by guides who not only speak the law, but live the law as well. We, therefore, need both the law and the one who delivers that law.

The need for a divinely inspired messenger is not merely based on the need for a message. While the message is crucial (as it regulates our way of life through the law), the necessity for a prophet is about man's need for a guide — a role model — as well as the leadership capable of implementing the law. This is why God has never sent a scripture without a messenger, yet many prophets have been sent without revealing a written scripture. This shows that sending a prophet is crucial and *independent* of scripture, not an *extension* of it. A prophet represents social and moral leadership, whereas scripture stands for the law.

Having established the need for messengers, we must then seek them by identifying a set of features they must possess to be chosen for the role. They include:

1. Having a calling toward the exclusive worship and reverence of the one true God. They themselves should be models of devotion and servitude to the Divine.

2. Enjoining virtues and exhibiting qualities like justice, kindness, charity, patience, gentleness, and affection.

3. Forbidding vices and combating superstitions, social evils, and corruption.

4. Exhibiting infallibility and moral excellence. This includes being truthful throughout their lives.

5. Providing indisputable proof of their prophethood.

Looking at the life of Mohammad son of Abdullah shows beyond any doubt that not only did he embody all of the above, but that he perfected and built upon the legacy of his predecessors who had delivered God's message.

Part Six

DIVINE LEADERSHIP

One of our fundamental tenets of belief pertains to the human family's enduring need for divinely appointed, righteous, unerring guides, or *Imams*. Today, the title 'Imam' is little more than a hackneyed term awarded to any Muslim cleric. Originally, however, the term was used only in reference to divinely pointed leaders.

Our faith places an immense emphasis on the concept of leadership and stress its central role in society. This is designed to prevent the emergence of false leaders and impostors. The reason for that is that with proper, qualified leaders, society can be steered in the right direction. Consequently, the selection process for a leader is one of the most rigorous to be found anywhere. In fact, it is so rigorous that only God can make that choice. This is one of the most unique aspects of our faith, which has led to Shia Muslim faith being named after this very concept; *Imamiyah*, meaning, 'those who follow their leaders'.

Here, two points need to be taken into account:

1. The need for divine leadership is not confined to the time of the Prophet. Leadership has relevance at all times and in every era. While prophets have ceased to exist following the demise of the Last Messenger, bringing to an end the era of divinely inspired apostles, has the need for enlightened leadership ended too? No one can claim that humanity no longer requires leaders who represent an extension to the heavenly message. If anything, the need for such leadership is more important now more than ever, given the explosion of temptations and corrupt political institutions, as well as an endless arsenal of weapons and our ability to inflict ever-greater harm on humanity and the environment. With more power comes greater risks of its misuse. Hence the need for sagacious and incorruptible leaders who can guide public life and illuminate the many dark spots we find along the way.

2. Because leadership occupies a pivotal role in society, the selection process for a leader in Shia Islam is one of the most rigorous. In fact, it is so exhaustive that only God can appoint a leader, just as God — *and only God* — appoints prophets. Thus, humankind's conceptions relating to this critical matter are simply irrelevant. We can prove this specific requirement through the following two arguments:

A) Logic: God's knowledge v. our inherent deficiency:

One of the attributes of a leader, just like a prophet, is being error-free. This means being pure from any sin, mistake, or fault. The problem is that we can never discern who among the masses fits this criterion, due to our shallow and extremely limited knowledge of what people are *really* like. The constant popular disappointment with our political leaders is but one proof of this. God, on the other hand, knows everyone better than they know themselves, and is the only one who can tell the good from the bad and the truthful from the sinful. Given the sensitive position of leadership, we need to be absolutely certain, and God alone is able to provide that certainty that allows us to recognize our leader without confusion.

B) Scripture:

Allah says in His holy book "Truly! On us is (to give) guidance."[28]

In this verse, the Exalted introduces Himself as the sole authority responsible for guiding humanity. Undoubtedly the best way for humankind to become acquainted with their religion and divine law is to follow a teacher and a guide appointed by God Himself, who may, in turn, lead people to their salvation. Therefore, the designation of the leader must lie exclusively with God.

Leadership from a Sunni[29] perspective

Sunni scholars are split over the issue of post-prophetic leadership into two main groups:

1) Those who claim that the Prophet died without appointing a successor for himself.[30]

2) Those who allege that even though the Prophet did

---

28. Quran 92:12

﴿إِنَّ عَلَيْنَا لَلْهُدَى﴾

29. A group of Muslims whose view of the concept of leadership led to the biggest schism in Islam.

30. Bukhari, Sahih, 8:126, and Sharh al Maqased 5:235

appoint Imam Ali as his heir, the people chose to remove him after the Prophet's death and pledged their allegiance tosomeoneelse.[31]

In response to the first group, we assert the previous points about God's justice. If God's religion is constant and unchanging, and if people are obligated to carry out His instructions, then it would be unjust for the guide to not appoint a teacher and to concurrently obligate that we follow his guidance. He must, therefore, appoint a guide, and thus He has.

To allege that the Prophet left his newfound nation, immature and fragile as it was, on its own, without providing any guidance on who (or on what basis) should lead, is an absurd assertion which contradicts logic as well as scripture.[32]

In response to the second group, we reply in two ways:

A) As established earlier, the leader of the nation must be the perfect embodiment and ideal epitome of the law; i.e. he must be infallible. Since people have no way of making that distinction, and have consistently erred in choosing a leader for themselves, they indeed replaced a jeweler with a shoemaker!

B) The Quran tells us, "It is not for a believer, man or

31. Ibn Abil Hadid, Nahjul Balagha 12:80. The author and others essentially claim that while the Prophet appointed a leader to succeed him, he merely nominated him and allowed the people the freedom to decide whether they wish to submit to him or not. However, in addition to the fact that the Prophet's words upon appointing his successor leave no room for such a flawed interpretation, this is an area that is an extension of divine leadership and much like Prophethood itself, as well as Salat, Hajj, fasting of Ramadan, and other religious injunctions, cannot be subject to consultation

32. For more on this, refer to Shirazi, Sultanu'l-Wa'izin, Peshawar Nights, and al-tijani-al-samawi, Then I Was Guided, as well as the many other (translated and original) polemical works on the subject.

woman, when Allah and His Messenger have decreed a matter that they should have any option in their decision."[33] It also states: "And your Lord creates whatsoever He wills and chooses, choice is not theirs."[34]

Regarding the issue of consultation[35] and the exchange of ideas: it is undoubtedly an important moral imperative in Islam, but consultation applies to subjects where God or His messenger has not issued a clear directive, and no injunction has been codified. If a clear directive exists, we must submit to it and strive to apply the will of God. Consultation on such matters is simply absurd.

The history of Islam screams loud and clear[36] that the Messenger of Allah carried out God's command on the 18th of Dhul-Hijjah, toward the end of the 10th year following the migration, at a site known as *Ghadeer Khum*, and took the hand of Ali (peace be upon him) in view of an audience exceeding one hundred thousand pilgrims, saying in a long and detailed sermon: "Whomsoever I am his master, Ali is his master."[37] The Prophet then prayed for those who would submit to Ali and support him and cursed his opponents and those who would reject him.

3) As we pointed out earlier, to create order in the life of humankind, God has instituted a complete and all-encompassing law, which applies until the last day of man's

---

33. Quran: 33:36

﴿وَ مَا كَانَ لِمُؤْمِنٍ وَ لَا مُؤْمِنَةٍ إِذَا قَضَى اللهُ وَ رَسُولُهُ أَمْرًا أَنْ يَكُونَ لَهُمُ الْخِيَرَةُ مِنْ أَمْرِهِمْ وَ مَنْ يَعْصِ اللهَ وَ رَسُولَهُ فَقَدْ ضَلَّ ضَلَالاً مُبِينًا﴾

34. Quran 28:68

﴿وَ رَبُّكَ يَخْلُقُ مَا يَشَاءُ وَ يَخْتَارُ مَا كَانَ لَهُمُ الْخِيَرَةُ سُبْحَانَ اللهِ وَ تَعَالَى عَمَّا يُشْرِكُونَ﴾

35. Known as '*Shura*', the notion that issues should be dealt with in a consultative process

36. *Ithbat al Hodat* 3:38, Ibn Abil Hadid, Shahr Nahjul Balaghah 2:289

37. «من كنت مولاه فعلي مولاه»

existence, owing to the fact that human nature is largely static and unchanging. An issue that might arise, however, is that even if we had the perfect and most detailed law, but not a knowledgeable expert to teach it, not only is there no guarantee of the law's application, but the law would be rendered entirely futile.

Take, for instance, driving a motor vehicle. Not only do we need an elaborate set of laws to govern this activity, but we also need police officers to ensure the rules are followed, and prevent any breaches from occurring by providing instructions to drivers. Without law enforcement officials, the laws are meaningless and would not achieve their purpose of establishing order.

In order to adhere to the law and apply it in their lives, people need individuals who represent the law. These are specially trained persons who know the law to the letter so they can relay that knowledge to those who cannot know it by their own accord. It is, therefore, a rational necessity to have such individuals who embody the law, as well as to prevent it from being violated.

Failing to appoint a leader for society while also obligating society to follow the law is like making university students go to class without appointing a professor to instruct them or a dean to manage them. It goes without saying that such an injunction is antithetical to justice.

Time and again, the Holy Prophet left instructions in no ambiguous terms regarding leadership after his death. One of the most reliable and famous statements is the tradition known as Hadith al Thaqalayn, in which the Messenger of Allah states: "I am verily leaving behind two weighty successors; the Book of Allah and my kindred, my progeny. If you hold on to them [both] you shall never go astray [as] God Has informed me that they will never separate until they return to me by the Pond (on Judgment Day)."[38]

With this momentous statement, the Prophet put the authority, infallibility, jurisdiction, and sovereignty of the Ahlulbayt on a par with that of the revealed book of God. The Quran itself highlights in no ambiguous terms the pivotal position of the People of the House. "Verily, God's wish is but to remove uncleanness far from you, O' People of the Household, and to purify you a (thorough) purifying"[39]

We thus conclude that God has appointed knowledgeable and infallible guides who are purified[40] from any and all sins and transgression in order to save mankind from the darkness of ignorance and corruption and lead them towards the path of happiness and perfection.

These individuals are the twelve divinely-appointed leaders, starting with the Commander of the Faithful Imam Ali (peace and blessings be upon him) and ending with the Proof of God, the Guided One: Imam Mahdi.

38. This narration (among many others) leaves no room for confusion as to the position of the Ahlulbayt – Holy Household of the Prophet, which is equal and on par with divine scripture. It means — among other extrapolations — that the Household are infallible and that they must be taken as leaders and guides, much like their counterpart, the book of Allah. Another fact extrapolated from this narration is the enduring presence of at least one member of the Prophet's progeny who fits the above description, hence the need for an infallible leader along with the Quran at all times.

39. Quran 33:33

40. As we will see in the next chapter

Part Seven

INFALLABILITY

One of the tenets of our creed is the immunity of prophets and Imams from any violation of divine law, as well as any kind of sin, mistake, or error. Divinely inspired leaders must be pure from any vices, blunders, or solecisms. Sunni scholars disagree, so we will respond to their viewpoint using rational arguments as well verses from the Holy Quran.

The rational argument involves contemplating the original purpose of sending prophets and appointing successors for them. The reason this is done is to introduce mankind to the religion of God in order for them to implement this religion in their lives. If, however, prophets and divinely-appointed leaders blundered or were guilty of dereliction of duty with regard to applying the law, the purpose of sending messengers would never be fulfilled. We also know that the action of an educator has a greater impact than his words. A Persian idiom states, *'greatness is not a matter of speech, for two hundred words are not worth a single deed'*. So if a teacher contradicts his words with his deeds, he will never succeed in educating.[41]

As for scriptural proof from the Holy Quran, Allah says: "When his Lord put Ibrahim to a test with certain Words, and he fulfilled them, He said, 'I am going to make you a leader for the people.' He said, 'And from among my progeny?' He replied, 'My covenant does not extend to the unjust.'"[42] Note that 'injustice' means three things in the Quran:

1) To associate partners to God: "Remember when Luqman said to his son, while he was advising him, 'My dear son, do not ascribe partners to Allah. Indeed, ascribing partners to Allah is grave injustice.'"[43]

2) Sins and transgressions: "Then We gave the Book as inheritance to such of Our slaves whom We chose. Then of them are some who commit injustice against themselves, and of them are some who follow a middle course, and of them are some who are, by Allah's Leave, foremost in good deeds. That is indeed a great grace."[44]

3) Oppression and inequity toward others: "We destroyed the generations before you when they were unjust; and their messengers came unto them with clear proofs but

41. Furthermore, one can state that,
A) without infallibility, the leader's credibility is in doubt and no part of his message or guidance can be deemed reliable. Everything he says or does, no matter how seemingly accurate, will not be taken as divine truth, and
B) he can no longer be adopted as a role model — a prime characteristic of a leader. Since his actions and words are prone to error, they cannot be emulated for those who seek certainty and perfection in their lives.

42. Quran 2:124

﴿وَإِذِ ابْتَلَى إِبْرَاهِيمَ رَبُّهُ بِكَلِمَاتٍ فَأَتَمَّهُنَّ قَالَ إِنِّي جَاعِلُكَ لِلنَّاسِ إِمَاماً قَالَ وَ مِنْ ذُرِّيَّتِي قَالَ لَا يَنَالُ عَهْدِي الظَّالِمِينَ﴾

43. Quran 31:13

﴿وَإِذْ قَالَ لُقْمَانُ لِابْنِهِ وَ هُوَ يَعِظُهُ يا بُنَيَّ لَا تُشْرِكْ بِاللهِ إِنَّ الشِّرْكَ لَظُلْمٌ عَظِيمٌ﴾

44. Quran 35:32

﴿ثُمَّ أَوْرَثْنَا الْكِتَابَ الَّذِينَ اصْطَفَيْنَا مِنْ عِبَادِنَا فَمِنْهُمْ ظَالِمٌ لِنَفْسِهِ وَ مِنْهُمْ مُقْتَصِدٌ وَ مِنْهُمْ سَابِقٌ بِالْخَيْرَاتِ بِإِذْنِ اللهِ ذَلِكَ هُوَ الْفَضْلُ الْكَبِيرُ﴾

they would not believe. Thus do We reward the guilty folk."[45]

In conclusion, a person who carries the burden of divine leadership must refrain from all three types of injustice cited above and be pure in the most sublime manner.

---

45. Quran 10:13

﴿وَ لَقَدْ أَهْلَكْنَا الْقُرُونَ مِنْ قَبْلِكُمْ لَمَّا ظَلَمُوا وَ جاءَتْهُمْ رُسُلُهُمْ بِالْبَيِّناتِ وَ ما كانُوا لِيُؤْمِنُوا كَذلِكَ نَجْزِي الْقَوْمَ الْمُجْرِمين﴾

Part Eight

MIRACLES

Miracles are actions performed by one who lays claim to prophethood or divine leadership. A miracle is, by definition, beyond the means of ordinary people, so much so that no one in any era can ever replicate or reproduce the act. While the term does not appear in the Holy Quran, it is mentioned in the prophetic narrations and has been alluded to in the Quran in the verse 'We have indeed sent Our messengers with Clear Signs',[46] which refers to something that validates the truthfulness and veraciousness of their claim.

As evidence for this belief, we refer to the fact that since prophets and Imams are guides and teachers for all of mankind, it is imperative that God introduce them to everyone — men and women, the educated as well as the unlettered — in a such a way that they can all know the prophet or Imam and not be lost or confused. This is also to prevent impostors and those ineligible for the role laying false claim

---

46. . Quran 57:25

﴿لَقَدْ أَرْسَلْنَا رُسُلَنَا بِالْبَيِّنَاتِ وَ أَنْزَلْنَا مَعَهُمُ الْكِتَابَ وَ الْمِيزَانَ لِيَقُومَ النَّاسُ بِالْقِسْطِ وَ أَنْزَلْنَا الْحَدِيدَ فِيهِ بَأْسٌ شَدِيدٌ وَ مَنَافِعُ لِلنَّاسِ وَ لِيَعْلَمَ اللهُ مَنْ يَنْصُرُهُ وَ رُسُلَهُ بِالْغَيْبِ إِنَّ اللهَ قَوِيٌّ عَزِيزٌ﴾

to this immensely sensitive position, just as identification documents are issued by agencies or companies exclusively to those deemed entitled to allow them to carry out their duties.

Let us thus refer very briefly to the everlasting miracle of the Messenger of Allah; the Quran. This holy book is considered a miracle for several reasons, the most important being its power of reason, its prophecies, and its scientific revelations. Consider a man living in an environment far from knowledge and culture, an orphan who lost both his parents at a young age, and never attended a class or wrote a single letter. It was in such circumstances that the Holy Prophet brought forth a set of facts in various scientific disciplines which, fourteen centuries on and after a technological revolution, scientists are only beginning to appreciate. This includes such astonishing discoveries as the rotation of the earth, the dual-sex nature of plants, the creation of humans from a man's sperm and woman's egg, and other important scientific facts which are detailed in specialized books on this subject.

Undoubtedly such a man is connected to the Creator of the world and all that exists, and his knowledge is invariably a matter of revelation and intuition, not deception or even personal speculation.

Part Nine

RESURRECTION

A fundamental tenet in our faith is belief in resurrection and the afterlife. It refers to the fact that mankind's life does not end with death, and that death is not synonymous with nothingness. Rather, it is a transition from one station to another, much like childbirth, which is a transition from a mother's womb into this world.

We also assert that after death, man shall see the results of his conduct and will be treated accordingly. We believe that after God recreates our body and injects our soul back into it, He will lead us to either heaven or hell, in order to face retribution or reward for our actions, be it good or bad.

To delve into this matter further we must discuss it from two perspectives:

Firstly, that death is not the cessation of life, and that belief in the next world is crucial.

Secondly, that God resurrects our bodies and places our souls within them once again, to allow us to see the conse-quences of our actions. This is referred to as the bodily *and* spiritual resurrection.

As for the first point, we can deduce it from two facts:

1. Having established God's justice, if life ends with death, that would constitute an injustice to those who lived a life of virtue and goodness and were deprived of many things in order to be good and righteous. Such people of good moral conduct had to refrain from satisfying their desires for the sake of a pure life, and yet without an afterlife their end would be equal to that of evildoers! What that means is that oppressors who never bothered with morality (i.e. God's law) or the rights of others would be ultimately on equal footing with those who are moral and ethical. This would be the equivalent of a teacher awarding good as well as bad students the same marks and, as we all know, this would be a gross act of injustice.

Belief in divine justice necessarily entails that life continues beyond this world until each person receives what they are due. Allah says, "Shall We, then, treat the obedient like the sinners? What is the matter with you? How do you judge?"[47]

He also states rhetorically, "Shall We make those who believe and do righteous deeds equal to those who commit mischief on the earth? Or shall We make the God-fearing equal to the sinners?"[48]

2) By acknowledging the infinite wisdom of God and that an act which has no purpose would never originate from Him, we conclude the following: if the universe and

---

47. Quran 68:35

﴿أَ فَنَجْعَلُ الْمُسْلِمِينَ كَالْمُجْرِمِينَ * مَا لَكُمْ كَيْفَ تَحْكُمُونَ﴾

48. Quran 38:28

﴿أَمْ نَجْعَلُ الَّذِينَ آمَنُوا وَ عَمِلُوا الصَّالِحَاتِ كَالْمُفْسِدِينَ فِي الْأَرْضِ أَمْ نَجْعَلُ الْمُتَّقِينَ كَالْفُجَّارِ﴾

all that exists — its incredible beauty, fathomless vastness, and enormous multitudes of things that it contains in order to facilitate man's life and welfare[49] — if He created all of this only to have it end abruptly and prematurely in death, after a lifetime of tribulation and struggle, is simply absurd! This would be like someone creating a farm, or building a factory by investing a great deal of money and putting in endless effort, waiting until the investment matures, only to destroy all the crop or produce! People of intellect would undoubtedly rebuke such a person, and see him worthy of berating for his foolish act. Any such undertaking and massive investment must be founded on a sensible and worthwhile purpose.

God's purpose for this world is the continuation of man's life. If our life was confined to this reality and if the outcome of our deeds is not reaped, would that not contravene basic wisdom? God states: "So did you think that We created you in vain, and that you will not be brought back to Us?"[50] God is, in fact, implying that without resurrection there would be no sensible point to this life whatsoever. Either there is a purpose and meaning to it all, or there must be nothing at all.

There must be a grand purpose beyond this life. In the grand scheme of things, no act of kindness will be of value to the doer unless it is properly rewarded, so all the great sacrifices made by the giants of human history, as well as those made by everyday men and women, would be futile as far as they are concerned without remuneration, which almost never occurs. Similarly, no act of aggression can be

---

49. Quran 14:32, 16:14, 32:27, etc.

50. Quran 23:115

﴿أَفَحَسِبْتُمْ أَنَّمَا خَلَقْنَاكُمْ عَبَثًا وَأَنَّكُمْ إِلَيْنَا لَا تُرْجَعُونَ﴾

deterred unless it can be adequately punished, and most such acts remain decisively *unpunished*. From the perpetual cycle of barbarous genocides and ruthless mass repressions, all the way down to the infinite, unnoticeable, personal injuries caused by fellow human beings, wrongdoing will almost always pass without so much as a slap on the perpetrator's wrist. Put that disturbing reality next to the grandeur and beauty of the universe and things just do not add up.

Regarding the second issue — that of resurrection involving our flesh and our spirit — once we have established that God has infinite power (as evidenced by His creation of the world) and reigns supreme over all things, it is not difficult to digest this tenet of the faith. The Holy Quran, in response to the objections of idolaters in Makkah as to the resurrection of both the body and soul, refers to examples of His limitless power. We will provide a few of those illustrations to our point:

1) The story of Abraham (peace be upon him) and the birds which were brought back to life in their bodies and then had their spirits injected into their flesh.[51]

2) The story of Ermya (some commentators have written his name as Uzair)[52]. Allah caused him to die for one hundred years, then resurrected him. All the while his food, composed of figs and grape juice remained fresh![53]

3) The story of the people of the cave who remained in a state of sleep for three hundred years or more. God states, "Thus did We make their case known to the people, that

---

51. See Quran 2:260

52. Often identified with the Judeo-Christian prophet Ezra

53. See Quran 2:259

they might know that the promise of Allah is true."[54] In other words, God did it to demonstrate His ability to resurrect the dead.

4) In various verses of the Holy Quran, Allah reminds us of the earth's death and subsequent blossoming of life through the four seasons. He states: "Then contemplate the tokens of Allah's Mercy! How He gives life to the earth after its death: verily the same will give life to the men who aredead."[55]

5) Sometimes the Quran explains that just as vegetation emerges from the midst of dirt, so do the dead emerge from the belly of the earth: "And [He] revives the earth after her death. And thus will you be brought out."[56]

6) At other times, the holy Quran speaks of man's return to life after death, and that this process is easier for God than man's initial creation, saying that "the One who creates from nothing is most certainly able to bring him back to life."[57]

There are further examples derived from verses throughout the Quran,[58] which prove the aforementioned points.

---

54. Quran 18:21

﴿وَ كَذٰلِكَ أَعْثَرْنا عَلَيْهِمْ لِيَعْلَمُوا أَنَّ وَعْدَ اللهِ حَقٌ﴾

55. . Quran 30:50

﴿فَانْظُرْ إِلٰى آثارِ رَحْمَتِ اللهِ كَيْفَ يُحْيِ الْأَرْضَ بَعْدَ مَوْتِها إِنَّ ذٰلِكَ لَمُحْيِ الْمَوْتٰى وَ هُوَ عَلٰى كُلِّ شَيْءٍ قَدِيرٌ﴾

56. Quran 30:19

﴿يُخْرِجُ الْحَيَّ مِنَ الْمَيِّتِ وَ يُخْرِجُ الْمَيِّتَ مِنَ الْحَيِّ وَ يُحْيِ الْأَرْضَ بَعْدَ مَوْتِها وَ كَذٰلِكَ تُخْرَجُونَ﴾

57. See Quran 30:27 and 36:79

58. See Quran 36:79

APPENDIX 1

Life of the late Ayatollah Alamolhuda

In my time as a seeker of knowledge, I have come to the realization that the single most precious thing in life is a learned and pious mentor. The moment you discover and connect with such a rare breed is a moment of veritable *coup de foudre*. Like a gasp of fresh air on meeting the water's surface, an erudite person can using little more than his words and conduct illuminate your world with newfound knowledge and wisdom. It is an incredibly humbling experience, yet, ironically, a spiritually uplifting encounter of the finest caliber.

One such person was the late Ayatollah Sheikh Baqer Alamolhuda. With a sense of humility reminiscent of the depth of his cognition, despite qualifications that rivaled giants of scholarship, he was a true gem in the midst of shiny but spurious pebbles. His cautious conduct, while a hallmark of all pious religious leaders, was in a class of its own. He was an impeccable educator, unrivaled debater, tenacious researcher, and a sincere and tireless adorer of the

Divine. Seeing him was a reminder that the more knowledge you possess, the more unassuming you must become.

In a world where trivial academic credentials are shamelessly flaunted for self-promotion, and where knowledge is almost never imparted without adequate remuneration, the character of this studious savant was bereft of such ignoble inclinations. His tone and facial expressions spoke of a man who had assiduously disciplined himself through decades of meditation and labor, turning him into a quintessential selfless slave.

His profound wisdom flowed effortlessly through his speech, and his demeanor was an ethics course in itself. Upon seeing him you were reminded of the narration in which Imam al-Sadeq quotes the Holy Prophet as saying,

"The disciples said to Jesus 'O Spirit of God! Whose company must we seek?' He said 'He whose appearance reminds of God, and whose speech increases your knowledge, and whose action makes you yearn for the hereafter".[59]

The Sheikh's singular focus was on the student's discipline, adopting a holistic approach to education. Thus, this produced a person encapsulated by religious teachings, mentally, spiritually, and intellectually.

In addition to being an expert in Islamic jurisprudence and

59. Al-Kulaini, Al-Kafi, 1:39:3

قَالَ رَسُولُ الله صلى الله عليه وآله: قَالَ الْحَوَارِيُّونَ لِعِيسَى عليه السلام: يَا رُوحَ الله مَنْ نُجَالِسُ؟ قَالَ: مَنْ يُذَكِّرُكُمُ اللهَ رُؤْيَتُهُ وَيَزِيدُ فِي عِلْمِكُمْ مَنْطِقُهُ وَيُرَغِّبُكُمْ فِي الْآخِرَةِ عَمَلُهُ.

theory, his primary field of expertise was Ma'aref, an expanding sphere that focuses on matters of credence and belief, extrapolated directly from primary sources. His teachers included the most eminent scholars in the Islamic seminary of Mashhad, such as Ayatollah Sayed Hadi Milani (in Fiqh and Usool), Ayatollah Sayed Mojtahedi Sistani (in philosophy and polemics), Ayatollah Mirza Hassan Ali Morvarid (in Fiqh and Ma'aref), Ayatollah Mirza Jawad Agha Tehrani, Ayatollah Sheikh Maleki Mianji Tabrizi, and Ayatollah Sheikh Ali Namazi (in Ma'aref).

Ultimately, he became a modern pillar of the school of the great 19th century reformist Ayatollah Mirza Mehdi Esfehani, a scholar whose challenging of the prevailing epistemic philosophical and mystical residue within some Shi'i schools continues to have seismic effects on theological circles. He fiercely advocated a return to the original unsullied teachings of the Quran and Ahlulbayt and cleansing the establishment from decaying theoretical frameworks developed by non-Islamic traditions, which, as he demonstrates in his works, run contrary to both creed and scripture.

Ayatollah Alamolhuda left a treasure trove of books, a large number of capable students, and a priceless collection of recorded lessons.[60] He was an example of how the Islamic seminaries can produce the finest human beings and that while secular institutions may be able to grant *information*, the Hawza produces true *knowledge*.

A prolific orator, a meticulous writer, and a sagacious mentor, the late Sheikh broke the hearts of those who had experienced his ephemeral presence when he passed away in 2008. After a brief illness, I watched as he succumbed to the will of his Lord with extraordinary submission.

May Allah bless the soul of Ayatollah Sheikh Alamolhuda and raise him with those whom he loved and served with utmost sincerity; the Holy Prophet and his immaculate Household (peace be upon them).

---

60. His written works include many titles in the field of Ma'aref and tackle some of the most critical subjects, and with a depth not often seen in traditional scholarly circles:

• *How Islam's Sun Shone* (six volumes) - An in-depth look at the moral dimensions of the Holy Prophet's character, which contributed to his success and led the masses to answer his call and embrace his message.

• *Perfection of the World* - What life will be like in the time of the reappearance of the Savior.

• *Bada'a; Sign of the Greatness of God* - An in-depth analysis of the concept of alteration of divine will

• *Knowing God* - A comprehensive epistemological exposition of knowing the divine.

• *A Response to those who reject the World of the Atom*

• *Intercession* - Three Volumes

• *Refuting Coercion and Delegation*

• *Blindness and Sight in the Narrations of Ahlulbayt*

• *Speech of the Soul in the Narrations of Ahlulbayt*

• *Exegesis of the Holy Quran According to Ahlulbayt* - Eighty-volume work (unpublished)

• *The Prophet and Ahlulbayt are One Light*

• *Hamza; Defender of Righteousness*

• *Epistemology; A Critique of Philosophy, Mysticism, and Materialism

APPENDIX 2

Religious Pluralism

Religious pluralism asserts that all religions are equally true. We are fundamentally opposed to it for the following reasons:

1) Religious pluralism is at odds with law of non-contradiction. Law of contradiction states: Two statements cannot both be true in the same sense at the same time.

We cannot say that "A is B" and "A is not B" simultaneously. These two statements are said to be mutually exclusive, and jointly exhaustive. It is, therefore, simply impossible for a statement and its negation to be jointly true.

2) Although world religions may share some similar underlying principles such as salvation, or belief in the afterlife, the differences in theology are not mere metaphors and symbology but rather solid contradictory differences. For example believing in Jesus as a manifestation of God is irreconcilable with the oneness and uniqueness of God, a notion Muslims take as a foundational tenet of their faith.

3) Any form of reconciliation between world religions would mean reducing each one down to find the lowest common denominator. To do so would require the removal of key tenets of each religious paradigm. However, it is impossible to reduce the world faiths down without compromising on key theological beliefs and totally eviscerating them of their true meanings.

Pluralism has a long history. Its origins can be found in Greek and Roman paganism. Within Greek mythology, syncretism was a common practice. The incorporation of "gods" and deities from other cultures into their own religion. They blended elements of Persian, Egyptian, Mesopotamian, and other pagan beliefs and practices into their own with a "Hellenistic" spin. The Romans did the same by bringing in the Greek gods and making them their own but with "Roman" names.

However, the current trend we see in pluralism; that is, the shift to a pluralist paradigm in contemporary society, is most certainly built from the foundations of the new postmodernist hegemony. The postmodernist claim is that there is no one "big T" truth, but rather truth, knowledge and ontological claims are all radically subjective and often constructed. They are only true relative to the context and the individual.

This postmodern paradigm has become rather prevalent in contemporary thinking, and often represent the underlying assumptions that many laypeople, particularly those living in western societies, have adopted, whether knowingly or otherwise. Consequentially, pluralism becomes very viable as a theology of religion. Each religion becomes "true" to the individual that has adhered to it, and has decided to use the credence and practices of said religion as a set of metaphors and symbols that represent the truth in the individual's own subjective way.

The prominent example used by famous Catholic pluralist John Hicks is that of an elephant bought into a room full of blind men who had never encountered an elephant before. They all touched the elephant, and one claimed the elephant was a snake (from touching the trunk), another claimed it was a pillar (from touching the leg).. etc. They ended up arguing, each claiming their account to be the truth... Hicks argues they are all true and each is referring to a limited aspect of the reality/truth.

The problem with such a claim is that some differences in these supposed "truths" are irreconcilably different! Is the universe eternal or not? Do we go through resurrection or reincarnation? Some of the differences in theology are so stark that they cannot be metaphors for the same thing in any shape or form.

Even in Abrahamic faiths, each religion has a different conceptualization of Jesus, each diametrically opposed to the other. In Judaism, he is seen as a false prophet, an impostor born out of wedlock, claiming to be the promised Messiah. In Christianity he is the son of God — indeed God himself — We cannot say he is both Son of God and not the son of God simultaneously, with both being true, or both reflecting "some aspect" of the truth. It is pure absurdity!

Furthermore, if we are to argue for pluralism, then we no longer have a right to call people to the religion of Islam. If we are all included on the path of salvation then why should we ask people to take such drastic changes in their lives, go through such difficult times and hardships as reverts and leave their religion (which is presumably another, equally valid, path to God).. and join my religion (which is merely another path to God too). Calling to the religion of Islam becomes redundant. In fact, being a Muslim is redundant, since everyone everywhere is on their path to salvation irrespective of their faith. Renouncing Islam, thus, becomes the best option since, as we pointed out earlier, being Muslim seems to be a rather painful experience in the world we live in.

There are numerous Quranic verses (such as 3:19-20 and 2:135-137), not to mention countless narrations assert that Islam is God's final message and that it came to negate all previous faiths, corrupted or not.

One may ask: Is it not possible that we could both be 'right' despite our deep theological differences? The Catholic church's dogma Extra Ecclesiam Nulla Salus (literally "no salvation outside the Church") denies any hope of salvation to the non-Catholic, let alone non-Christian. The same is true of Judaism and almost every other faith tradition. Pluralists argue that the only hope for achieving social harmony is to adopt a strictly pluralistic approach. They claim that religious exclusivism objects to fraternizing between different religious vocabularies for anxiety for creedal purity. But that could not be farther from the truth. Believing that Islam is the one true path does not mean we deny commonalities with other faiths. We firmly acknowledge that all the major theistic traditions claim that humanity as a whole has a knowledge of God in some form or another, and that a perfect ignorance of God is impossible for any people. For another, one can insist on absolutely inviolable demarcations between religions at every level only at the price of painfully unrefined accounts of what each tradition teaches.

However, we assert that one should not try to dissolve disparate creeds into one another, much less into some vague syncretistic, doctrinally vacuous "spirituality". Pluralists trying to confuse syncretism with pluralism which is a big mistake. We can live in absolute peace and harmony without total assimilation. We need not take all contradictory religious teachings as one, in order to accept the humanity of the other. This is why Imam Ali states unequivocally:

> *"People are either your brothers in faith, or your equals in creation".*

This cardinal rule shows that there is absolutely no tolerance towards racism, bigotry, or violence in Islam, yet we can still maintain that we follow the truth and that others, while demonstrably wrong, share our humanity and, thus, deserve our equitable and harmonious treatment.

Made in the USA
San Bernardino, CA
05 April 2016